YO-BQW-685

HAIKU REFLECTIONS

BOOKS BY THE AUTHOR

Poetry:

Haiku Reflections
ISBN–Hard: 0–918340–07–1

Idylls of the Seasons
ISBN–Hard: 0–918340–06–3

Lisping Leaves
ISBN–Hard: 0–918340–03–9

Self-help:

Easy Steps to Correct Speech
ISBN–Hard: 0–918340–00–4

Easy Steps to Good Grammar
ISBN–Hard: 0–918340–01–2

Easy Steps to a Large Vocabulary
ISBN–Hard: 0–918340–04–7

Little Stepping Stones to Correct Speech
ISBN–Hard: 0–918340–02–0

Pasaderitas Hacia el Ingles Correcto
ISBN–Hard: 0–918340–05–5

HAIKU

REFLECTIONS

by

Ida R. Bellegarde

60236

Bell Enterprises, Inc.   Pine Bluff, Arkansas

Library of Congress Catalog Card No. 78–72586
ISBN—Hard: 0-918340-07-1

BELL ENTERPRISES, INC.

Post Office Box 9054   Pine Bluff, Arkansas 71611

DEDICATION

to

my petite niece, Paula Ruth Groves

CONTENTS

Spring

SPRINGTIME

Low whispery trills
of a mocker in springtime . . .
amorous wooing.

ZERO HOUR

Life really begins
when springtime voices of the wind
are singing madly.

THE RETURNING

Quivering delight:
swallows riding on the wind . . .
gay anticipation.

DARK RAGE

Riding on the wind . . .
rain clouds flinging gray tendrils
like misty climbing vines.

MARCH WINDS

Joy comes easily
on a windy day in March . . .
passionate delight.

MISTY MOVEMENT

Gossamer flowing . . .
a hummingbird's restless wings . . .
a spring breeze blowing.

INTERLUDE

In early morning hours
the echoing thunder
brings sparkling showers.

WINDY LAKE

Lake waters come alive . . .
whispering and chuckling
in rippling, whiffling winds.

HARBINGER

Spring beauties peeking
through tawny winter grass . . .
fast fleeing winter.

ACCOLADE

Shouting frog voices
after a frozen slumber . . .
joyous grateful applause.

LILACS IN BLOOM

Fragrance everywhere . . .
   Lavender lilacs spilling
      pungent perfume on the air.

HERALDING SPRING

Billowing white clouds
   tangled in distant pine trees . . .
      heralding springtime.

ENTHUSIASM

Excited booming
   of April thunder echoing . . .
      elation looming.

JUBILATION

Loud bursts of white spray . . .
   laughing plum trees flaunting skirts
      of flimsy frothy lace.

ANNOUNCING SPRING

The saffron trumpet flower
cascading from budding trees . . .
a broadcasting bower.

LYRICAL IMPATIENCE

Impatient trilling
of frogs in early springtime
make heady music.

SPRING RAIN

Over the meadow
  crystal raindrops chase the wind . . .
  life is wonderful.

QUIETUDE

A lyrical stream
  singing in the gentle moonlight . . .
  tranquil peace tonight.

FRENZIED CALLING

Nature's most impassioned ways . . .
   eagerness personified . . .
      the bugling of jays.

DELIGHTFUL BLISS

Springtime happiness:
   clouds racing before the wind . . .
      bird-songs from the trees.

PROTECTION

Purple modesty . . .
the violet's shy humility . . .
royal panoply.

FASHION OF SPRING

Green willow twigs . . .
slender and tall, and misting . . .
spring's emerald wigs.

DARING CONFIDENCE

The gallant cardinal
  with fluttering scarlet crest . . .
   flaming arrogance.

SPRING THAW

Riling, roiling waters . . .
  violent destructive power
   of an angry river.

MORNING ENCHANTMENT

Morning enchantment . . .
the rapture of honeysuckle
on a friendly breeze.

CHICANERY

Gray and gloomy days . . .
the chill and cheerless weather . . .
April's trickery.

PLUM BLOSSOMS

On the misty air,
   spicy fragrance of plum trees
     foaming in early dawn.

FOOTPRINTS

Tender misty rain . . .
   timid sunshine's dusty gold . . .
     footprints of early spring.

AMETHYST SANCTUARY

Purple gossamer . . .
the redbud's lavender mist
in a woodland cove.

SYMBOLS OF LOVE

Violets are blooming . . .
purple symbols of romance,
and springtime wooing.

APPLE BLOSSOMS

Snowflakes in the spring . . .
   faded blossoms from apple trees
   frosting the ground.

PEACH BLOSSOMS

Like a rosy banner . . .
   a pink tide of peach blossoms
   streaming on the wind.

HONEYSUCKLE

Unendurable . . .
  the fragrance of honeysuckle
  on the morning air.

THE MIMOSA

A strange exotic scent
  rode on the winds from the south . . .
  mimosa blossoms.

SPRING BEAUTIES

A carpet of white,
   landscaping the meadow . . .
      spring beauties' saucy smiles.

LILACS

Dewy flower heads . . .
   giant bouquets of purple lilacs
      breathe upon the air.

NONCHALANCE

Spring comes wandering,
while winter's snow still lingers
in roadside gullies.

EARLY SPRING

Gay discovery:
greening spikes of iris,
reaching for the sunlight.

MAY

Melodious May:
   the trilling of the mocker,
   and the lively wind.

DEPARTURE

Retreating winter . . .
   when pine trees become wind chimes
   to herald the spring.

RESTITUTION

A passionate wind,
   warming the frozen marshland . . .
   nature's recompense.

REIMBURSEMENT

Moving listlessly
   through a dreamy morning in May . . .
   life's gentle reward.

INEXPERIENCE

A gusting young wind,
   not yet knowing its mind,
   makes an amusing day.

SERENITY

A greening meadow
   laced with the odors of spring . . .
   a spiritual thing.

ETERNAL SPRING

Restless air pulsing
with new life and growing things . . .
spring springs eternal.

QUIET PEACE

Merry tinkling sounds
of tiny frogs in springtime . . .
celestial peace.

Summer

FLAMING SILHOUETTES

At the vesper hour,
   the golden sun in the west
   paints hilltop-silhouettes.

LETHARGY

In a whimsical lagoon,
   blessed peace
   out where water lilies bloom.

MIDSUMMER MAGIC

Softly the dream waves begin . . .
   drowsy blue waters
     moving with the wind.

SUMMER MELODY

The mockingbird's song
   with passionate summer lilt . . .
     trilling all night long.

DAWN

Softly the eastern sky
  catches the rosy glow
    of approaching dawn.

WHITE PHLOX

Perfume on the breeze . . .
  sweet fragrance of white phlox
    lingers through the summer.

THE GARDEN

Dew-drenched and lovely,
   the garden spills upon the air
   essence of roses.

SINGING SILENCES

Singing silences . . .
   gentle summer fragrances
   in a shaded cove.

FAIRY MUSIC

Like fairy music:
the tinkle of tiny waves.
in a prattling brook.

GRANDEUR

Great golden masses,
gilded by the western sun . . .
evening thunderheads.

BLARING TRUMPETS

The trumpet creeper shouts
from waving topmost branches . . .
flamboyant blossoms.

EVENING QUIET

Gently radiant,
starlight and deepening sky . . .
hushed softness at dusk.

A LONELY CALL

The cry of tree toads
in a darkening woodland
is a bitter-sweet call.

COLOR CONTRAST

On a scarlet phlox
black and yellow butterflies
settle serenely.

UNRIVALED

Unique perfection:
  cumulus wind-sculptured clouds
  riding high above.

STILLNESS AT DUSK

Pensive quiet twilights:
  dense green summer foliage,
  cloistered quiesence.

QUIET PEACE

Dreamy contentment:
   cattle moving lazily
     over summer pastures.

NATURE'S DELIGHT

Close to paradise:
   airy plumes of misty cloud
     loitering in the sky.

WINDY DAY

The day had its day:
  shrill winds dwindled into silence
  as twilight falls.

SUMMER DELIGHT

A soul-stirring sight:
  a proud flaunting treetop
  against an azure sky.

RENDEZVOUS

Amorous calling:
the trilling of a cricket
in a nocturn rendezvous.

THE PASSING

In dying grasses
I heard a cricket singing . . .
farewell to summer.

QUIET BEAUTY

A thing of beauty
among nature's repertoire . . .
a breeze-swept willow.

TRANQUILIZER

A soft soothing sound:
the gentle slurring of the wind . . .
nature's sedative.

THE SYMBOL

Hallmark of excellence:
a soft whisper of fragrance
on a summer breeze.

MORNING MAGIC

The murmuring pines,
dew-lacquered needles glinting
in early sunbeams.

ON STAGE

Summer's bright newness:
   thespian perfection
   in nature's sweeping drama.

SUMMER SYMPHONY

Summer symphony:
   a frog chorus in early dawn . . .
   enthralling cellos.

Autumn

TRANSIENT BEAUTY

When sunlight fails,
    shadows linger like purple magic
      in the hills at twilight.

AUTUMN TWILIGHT

The sad keening of the wind
    is soft and gentle . . .
      twilight in autumn.

THE DAWN OF FALL

Autumn days are near:
   the pale sun spreads long fingers
   through purple shadows.

SIMPLICITY

I have a need for:
   the sound of rain in the trees,
   and a sighing breeze.

ALONE

Autumn's sole breeze . . .
  floating in and out of trees,
  making sad music.

WANDERING WINDS

Effortlessly gliding,
  endlessly wandering . . .
  seeking the elusive dream.

TINKLING BELLS

Soft musical sounds:
   tiny trills like tinkling bells . . .
   little birds calling.

THE END OF FALL

All life is silenced:
   no birds sing from the treetops,
   and a west wind grieves.

ADJUSTMENT

A disturbing truth:
   shrill screams of a hunting hawk . . .
   nature's counterbalance.

MOBILITY

Gentle swirling mist
   moving in on the restless breeze . . .
   a lively white shadow.

APPROACHING FALL

Only the faint echoes
of a drumming woodpecker . . .
the essence of fall.

LATE AUTUMN

The year is dying:
the wind's eternal sighing
in the leafless trees.

Winter

RECOMPENSE

In the ghostly fog
　　the white sun's crystal halo . . .
　　　　winter's atonement.

WHITE BEAUTY

Snow showers in winter . . .
　　the drooping pine trees festooned
　　　　in snowy white plumes.

SORROW

At midnight, sadly,
  low moaning in the eaves . . .
    the grieving frigid wind.

PROPHECY

A gentle restless sky,
  white clouds forming in the east,
    forecast an early spring.

WINTER'S BENEFICENCE

The deepening silence
  of a dark winter-woodland
    is balm for the weary.

WINTER WONDERLAND

Softly falling snowflakes
  glistening like diamonds
    on the moonbeam-silvered snow.

FRIGID MELODY

Savage winter winds
　　make a phantom melody
　　　　across the frozen snow.

WINTER FURY

A driving sleety snow,
　　and a howling wintry blast
　　　　make snug a roaring fire.

SILHOUETTES

Stark winter shadows:
   black silhouettes against the snow . . .
   the leafless oak trees.

SILENT WOODLAND

Nothing surpasses
   the silence of a woodland
   in deep winter days.

NIGHTTIME BRILLIANCE

Cold brittle brilliance:
bright evening star swinging high
over frozen fields.

WINTER MUSIC

Cold cascading winds
make a wispy pleasant sound
when winter speaks softly.

DATE DUE